FORTY REASONS I AM A CATHOLIC

FORTY REASONS

REASONS

I AM A̅ CATHOLIC

PETER KREEFT

SOPHIA INSTITUTE PRESS

Manchester, New Hampshire

Sophia Institute Press
Box 5284, Manchester, NH 03108
1-800-888-9344

www.SophiaInstitute.com

Sophia Institute Press® is a registered trademark of Sophia Institute.

Library of Congress Cataloging-in-Publication Data

Names: Kreeft, Peter, author.
Title: Forty reasons I am a Catholic / Peter Kreeft.
Description: Manchester, New Hampshire : Sophia Institute Press, 2018.
Identifiers: LCCN 2017058117 | ISBN 9781622826148 (pbk. : alk. paper)
Subjects: LCSH: Catholic Church — Apologetic works.
Classification: LCC BX1752 .K745 2018 | DDC 282 — dc23 LC record available at https://lccn.loc.gov/2017058117

7th printing

*Please pray for the eternal happiness of
Brand Blanshard and Albert Camus, two honest
atheists who helped me become a better Catholic.*

CONTENTS

〜

FORTY REASONS I AM A CATHOLIC

INTRODUCTION

Since I have ADD and get bored very easily, I believe books should be short. Since introductions are almost always boring, I also believe introductions should be short.

My title explains itself. But it is misleading: there are more than forty reasons. In fact, there are at least ten to the eighty-second power, which (I am told) is the number of atoms in the universe. And that's just in ordinary matter, which makes up only 4.9 percent of the universe, the rest being dark matter (26.8 percent) and dark energy (68.3 percent).

Each of my reasons is an independent point, so I have not organized this book by a succession of chapters or headings. Most readers remember only a few "big ideas" or separate points after reading a book anyway. I've never heard anyone say, "Oh, that was a good continuous-process-of-logically-ordered-argumentation" or "Oh, that was a good multiple-headed-and-subheaded-outline," but I've often heard people say, "Oh, that was a good point."

"Why are you a Catholic?" is a good question.

The Catholic Faith is not the default position anymore anywhere in the world, as it was in Christendom during the Middle Ages, and perhaps it was never supposed to be.

A good question deserves a good answer.

Here are forty of mine.

1

BECAUSE I BELIEVE THAT CATHOLICISM IS TRUE

I am Catholic because I believe that Catholicism is true. It seems obvious to me that to believe that something is true is the first and only honest reason for anybody ever to believe anything.

If that is not obvious to you, if that is not your very first reason for believing whatever you believe, then I think you are not being totally honest with yourself.

Do you disagree with that? Does that seem too tough-minded? Let's test it with a thought experiment.

Imagine you are God at the Last Judgment, and you have to decide the eternal fates of two people. One is a dishonest Christian, and the other is an honest atheist. Let's not even consider Hell; let's assume both can get to Heaven, but one needs more Purgatorial correction and preparation than the other.

Which person would you see as needing the more serious Purgatory? Or, if you cannot even imagine a Purgatory, which person would you see as meriting the higher place in Heaven, or able to endure more of Heaven's truth?

One of them said that he believed Catholic Christianity even though he didn't think it was true, or perhaps didn't even *care* whether it was true, but embraced it for some other reason: either because his friends believed it, or because it made him feel good, or because it was advantageous for his earthly life in some other way. Let's give him the benefit of the doubt and ascribe to him the two best and most important motives in the world other than truth—namely morality and happiness. Let's say he embraced Catholicism not because it was true but because it made him happy or because it made him more moral. What do you think a perfect God would say to that?

I think He would say that happiness without truth is not true happiness and therefore is not truly happiness at all; and that morality without truth is not true morality and therefore is not truly morality at all. Therefore, he needs and deserves a more basic correction than the honest atheist. And I think you would have to agree.

If you still disagree, try another thought experiment. Turn back the clock and remember yourself at the age of three on December 24. You probably believed in Santa Claus, and this belief probably made you significantly more moral, or at least you behaved more morally. You were also happier because of this belief. Now you no longer believe in Santa Claus. Why not? For one reason only: because you are honest and therefore do not want to believe what is not true, even if that belief gives you other benefits that are very significant, such as moral goodness and happiness (which are certainly two of the greatest of all goods).

I appeal, therefore, to your tough-minded honesty, which you have just proved you have by your reaction to my two thought experiments.

Honesty treats truth as a nonnegotiable absolute.

If you are not a Catholic, please do *not* become one unless and until you honestly believe that Catholicism is true. If you are a Catholic for any other reason than Catholicism's truth — if you believe that Catholicism is untrue, or probably untrue, but you are a Catholic anyway; or if you simply do not even care about whether it is true — then please question your motives and your honesty, and then question your religion. And if this honesty causes you to leave the Church, please do. Thomas Aquinas says that remaining in the Church even though you believe it is false is a mortal sin, a sin of hypocrisy, a sin against the absolute of honesty, a sin so serious that it is sufficient matter for eternal damnation if not repented of. On the other hand, if you leave the Church, you are making a mistake, but if it is an honest mistake; and if your motive is the search for truth, God will bless you and your quest by rewarding your search and bringing you back to the truth. ("Seek and you will find" [Matt. 7:7].)

As for me, I believe that Catholicism is true, and that is why I am a Catholic.

2

BECAUSE IT'S THE BEST OF FIVE CHOICES

There are many religions in the world. Why did I choose to be a Catholic? Here are the steps in my reasoning.

My first choice was between religion and no religion. *Religion* means a "yoke" or a "binding-back relationship." Religion is a relationship with God. (*God* here is taken in the broadest sense as at least some higher power, something greater than us.) So, an atheist is one who believes that there is no God at all, and therefore there ought to be no religion at all.

The arguments against atheism are well known. The two that are mentioned in the Bible are

1. The evidence in nature: Who made it? Did the "Big Bang" just happen for no reason or cause? And why is it so intelligently designed?

2. The absoluteness of conscience: Why is it always morally wrong to disobey your conscience deliberately? Where did it get that absolute authority if it didn't come from God but only from chance, genetics,

9

evolution, society, or your parents, none of which are infallible?)

The two basic reasons I'm not an atheist are not my mother and father, but my conscience and my universe.

My next choice was between one God and many gods. Polytheism is not a live option today. It's almost totally dead. I've never met a polytheist. In fact, in one sense, polytheism never existed, because behind all the many gods of polytheism we almost always find one supreme God. Something or Somebody must be Number One. There can't be two absolutely absolute absolutes.

My next choice was between the God of the Bible, who personally created the universe, and the god of pantheism (the god of Upanishadic Hinduism, or the cosmic "Buddha mind," or the Tao, or "the Force" of "Star Wars"), which is not a superhuman person with a moral will but just a nameless mind or force or ideal.

One reason for preferring biblical theism to pantheism is that the pantheist's God is everything, and therefore is evil as well as good. I cannot love or worship or guide my life by a god who has a "dark side," who is half evil or indifferent to good and evil.

Another reason for theism over pantheism is that only the God of the Bible (of Judaism and Christianity and Islam) unites what have always been the two deepest instincts in the human heart—namely, the religious instinct and the moral instinct. We are morally responsible to this God.

My next choice, once this God is accepted, is whether to accept or reject Jesus' claim to be divine, to be the Son of this God. That is the essence of Christian theology, as distinct from Jewish or Islamic.

I cannot get around the "Lord, liar, or lunatic" argument. If Jesus is not divine, then He was the maddest madman or the most blasphemous egomaniac who ever lived; not the best of men but the worst. "I'm divine; worship me; trust me with your soul's eternal salvation. I am perfect. It was I who designed your universe and your soul." Has anyone in history ever told a bigger lie than that?

If that's who He really was (either liar or lunatic), then who invented the Jesus of the Gospels, who is the polar opposite of both a liar and a lunatic: honest, altruistic, passionate, wise, practical, creative, saintly, and fascinating? That last adjective is the most telling one because it is impossible to imitate successfully. Once you get to know them, lunatics are never really fascinating, and neither, once they become familiar, are lying egomaniacs. Even if Jesus is totally fictional, He is the most fascinating and compelling literary figure in human history. Who invented Him? If He is fictional, who invented that new genre of realistic fantasy twenty centuries before Tolkien? A bunch of peasant Galilean fishermen?

The next choice was about the claim of the Catholic Church to be the Church Christ founded and authorized. This was harder for me, since I was brought up as a Protestant. But the historical record of the Catholic Church's continuity in doctrine, in apostolic succession, and in her belief in the Eucharistic Real Presence for two thousand years is data too massive to ignore or explain away. If I was going to be a Christian, I had to be where Christ Himself wanted me to be, in the thing He Himself created for me as my spiritual home and as the instrument of His teaching authority. And the Bible itself tells us that that thing is not just the Bible but the Church.

So, the links in the chain are: (1) religion, not atheism; (2) monotheism, not polytheism; (3) theism, not pantheism; (4) Christianity, and therefore Trinitarianism, not Unitarianism;

and (5) Catholicism, not Protestantism. Or, (1) Higher Power, (2) One, (3) Creator, (4) Christ, (5) Church.

The three most important links in this chain are the last ones: that the material universe is God's creation, Christ is God's incarnation, and the Church is Christ's body.

All that is not yet quite a *proof* but is the map of a journey, which can also be the map of a proof, i.e., a justification of the journey, an obeying of the first pope's command to "be prepared to make a defense [of] the hope that is in you" (1 Pet. 3:15). The details of that justification are in many good books of apologetics.

3

BECAUSE JESUS IS REALLY, TRULY, PERSONALLY, LITERALLY PRESENT IN EVERY CONSECRATED HOST IN THE WORLD

Jesus is available to me in His body and in His soul in every Mass, in my body and in my soul. And I need Him.

There is a little red light burning perpetually in the sanctuary of every Catholic church in the world except from Good Friday until the Easter Vigil, between the time Jesus died on the Cross and the time He rose from the dead on Easter morning. That light means that Jesus is really there, fully alive, and fully present; that there is a consecrated Host in the tabernacle. It is like the light that the father of the prodigal son probably kept burning in the front window of his home every single night while his beloved son was gone, so that when his son came back, he could see that light and know that that was still his home and that he was welcome back and that his father was still waiting for him.

I am God's prodigal son, and I need to come home, and home is wherever Jesus is, and *He is there*. That is why I have to go there: because I need to fall at His feet in repentance and adoration and unutterable joy.

Do you doubt that He is there? If so, I have an experiment for you to do, not just think about doing. This applies to you whether you are a non-Catholic or a Catholic who doubts the Real Presence. (There are doubters in both camps.) Just go into a Catholic church sometime when nobody else is around to see you, and kneel in the front pew or at the Communion rail, and pray, with all honesty: "God, is that You? Are You really there? If not, please don't let me believe that lie. Don't let me be a Catholic. Because I want to know and live the truth, whatever it is. And if You *are* there, please draw me there. Send Your Holy Spirit to inspire me to believe, so that I can be where You are. Make me a Catholic. For the very same reason: because I want to know and live the truth, whatever it is."

It's parallel to the prayer of the skeptical agnostic: "God, I honestly don't know whether You exist, but I want to know the truth and live the truth, so if You do exist, please convince me that You do, in Your time and in Your way."

Only three things could possibly be reasons for not praying either of those prayers.

One of them is absolute certainty that that religious idea is false and that those billions of saints, sages, mystics, and ordinary people like you were all really, really stupid for believing it. That's arrogance.

The second reason is not caring whether this tremendous, life-changing claim is true. That's indifference, not giving a damn about truth.

The third reason is the fear that it *is* true. That's one step from conversion.

4

BECAUSE THE CATHOLIC RELIGION IS FROM GOD, NOT JUST FROM MAN

The Catholic Church is God's gift of a divine revelation of truth that comes to us with divine and not just human authority. His gift of forgiveness and salvation also comes with divine authority.

That claim is like the claim of religious Jews to be "God's chosen people." It is either true or false. If the claim is true, it explains their survival, their uniqueness, their achievements, and their wisdom. It is the humblest possible interpretation of the data that it is God's doing, not theirs. The only alternative—that it is not God's doing but their own—is the most arrogant, egotistic racist lie any people ever foisted on the world. It is also blasphemy because their whole prophetic tradition claims, "Thus says the Lord" for mere human thinking.

But if that is the case, if there is no God behind it all, how can we account for the facts? Everyone wants to kill them, from

Pharaoh to Haman to Hitler, yet they not only survive but thrive. Everyone wants to convert them, yet they remain true to their ancestral traditions for more than three thousand years, lovingly preserving their scriptures in which God condemns them for apostasy and infidelity and stubbornness.

So, whatever they are, whether they are God's chosen people or not, they are not just another people, not just one among many equals. They are the exception to every law of history. They are different. They are unique. They are the iron ball in the pit of the world's stomach that it can neither digest nor disgorge.

The Church's claim about herself is like the Jews' claim about themselves.

It is also like Christ's claim about Himself: that He is not just a human person but a divine Person, the only-begotten eternal Son of God. If that is not true, it is the most arrogant, egotistic, blasphemous lie or the most literally insane self-delusion ever uttered by human lips. A mere man who claims to be God is either a madman or a devil. He is certainly not just a good man.

But if he is a madman or a devil, how can we account for His wisdom, His love, and His holiness?

So, whoever He is, He is not just another good man, one among many equals.

Similarly, the Catholic Church's claim to be the one true, authoritative, visible Church that Christ Himself founded and authorized to teach His truth, in His name, with His infallible authority — this claim is either true or false, and if it is false, it is the wickedest, most arrogant, and most blasphemous claim any religious body in the world has ever made.

But if that is the case, how to account for her wisdom, her holiness (her saints), her survival, and her fidelity to Christ's teachings through two thousand years of history?

So, whatever it is, the Catholic Church is not just another "denomination," one among equals. She is unique. Like Christ. Like the Jews. Like their God.

5

BECAUSE OF THE UNPRECEDENTED HISTORICAL FACT THAT THE CHURCH HAS NEVER ONCE LOWERED HER STANDARDS, NEVER CHANGED HER TEACHING

Catholic dogmas have remained pure even when the teachers were impure. Even when the Borgia popes not only did not love the poor but took advantage of them and oppressed them for the sake of greed and gold, they continued to teach Christ's command to love the poor, and His prophetic curses on oppressors and on greed.

But what of the Church's sins and stupidities? What of the jackasses who have "run" this very earthly "business"? One of her first bishops was Judas Iscariot! And still today, some bishops are craven compromisers who care more about their reputation than about horribly abused children. Most bishops and priests are good and honest men, but only a very few are saints and heroes.

Hypocrisy, it is said, is "the tribute that vice pays to virtue." That tribute included accurately defining hypocrisy and faithfully condemning it. Jesus condemned the Pharisees' hypocrisy unsparingly, but he agreed with their theology. They did not practice what they preached (boo!), but at least they preached what they did not practice (hurray!).

Like the Jews of the Old Testament, like the Pharisees of Jesus' day, the Church does not compromise her high and holy standards and teachings even when she is manned by craven cowards and compromisers. That is nothing less than a miracle. What other visible institution has refused to change its teachings or lower its demands that all must practice both loving-kindness and moral heroism even when the institution is manned by cruel cynics and moral weaklings? Even when her crusaders were hating, slaughtering, and pillaging in the name of Christ, it was in the name of the Christ who commanded love, peace, and altruism. Their behavior did not change and lower Christ; Christ eventually changed and raised their behavior.

That Christ should entrust His mission to such jackasses is astonishing — as was His choice of that same beast to carry Him into the holy city to do His holiest work, on the Cross. He continues to have the same strange choice of vehicles.

When Napoleon kidnapped Pope Pius VII, he said to him, "We will destroy your Church." The Pope laughed and replied, "If we Catholics haven't been able to do that for nineteen hundred years, you won't either."

6

FOR THE SAME REASON
G. K. CHESTERTON GIVES:
TO GET MY SINS FORGIVEN

Nearly all the Church Fathers call the Church "the ark"—the ark of salvation. Noah's family was hardly a holy family (read the record!) but they had the sense to get aboard the ark.

But why do we need the Church to get our sins forgiven? Because Christ promised, not to all His disciples but only to His apostles (who ordained their successors by a definite sacramental act, "the laying on of hands"), that the sins they forgave on earth would be forgiven in Heaven (John 20:23; Matt. 16:19).

When I go into the confessional, I become a fundamentalist, or at least an archconservative: I need to be absolutely certain that the priest's words of forgiveness, which he repeats not in his own name but in the name of Jesus Christ, are literally true and divinely guaranteed. If you don't think you need that, you are either a fool or a person far holier than the saints.

Once I stop fooling myself, I realize that I don't really know God very well at all; but I know four other things very well.

1. I know myself (again, once I stop fooling myself), and I know I am an inveterate sinner and need to get my sins forgiven.

2. I also know, from the Bible, that Jesus claimed the authority and therefore the power (authority is "right making might," not "might making right") to forgive sins. That is one of the reasons the Jews rightly perceived that He was claiming divinity: "Who but God alone can forgive sins?" (Luke 5:21).

3. I also know, from the passages in the Gospels quoted above, that Jesus gave this authority and power to His apostles and (from Acts 1:22, 14:23, 16:4, Titus 1:5, and from subsequent Church history) that these apostles passed this apostolic authority on to their successors (apostolic succession) through the laying on of hands in the sacrament of Holy Orders (Acts 8:18; 1 Tim. 4:14). These successors are the bishops and priests of the one Catholic (universal) Church.

4. I also know that this apostolic Church, both in the Roman West and in the Orthodox East, is the only church that both claims to have and does have apostolic succession in her priesthood and has the sacrament of Confession and has priests who have the authority to forgive sins — my sins.

When free air transportation is available, why choose to walk?

7

BECAUSE THE CATHOLIC CHURCH HAS BEEN INFALLIBLY RIGHT ABOUT EVERYTHING SHE HAS EVER CLAIMED TO BE INFALLIBLY RIGHT ABOUT

The Catholic Church has been infallibly right about everything she has ever claimed to be infallibly right about. And that has been true even when everybody else has been wrong. In fact, especially then.

- She has been right, with Augustine, about the relation between the Church and the State. Church and State are expressions of but are not identical with Augustine's two "cities," the opposite communities of believers and unbelievers, their identity known only to God. Members of these two cities or communities share a common human nature and common human needs and values, such as justice and order and law and man's natural, earthly goods, and that fact constitutes the basis for the Church's loyalty to the State. But the two cities are opposed about man's ultimate good, and therefore the Church will not compromise her religion even if it means martyrdom. When the State becomes a religion, the Church becomes its enemy.

• She has been right about war, blessing but not requiring Gandhian nonviolence and allowing but not glorifying war but only the defensive goings-to-war that are just and necessary.

• She has been right about the Trinity, avoiding every heresy: Arianism, Docetism, Tritheism, Unitarianism, Apollinarianism, Monothelitism, Monophysitism, Nestorianism, Patripassianism, Sabellianism, Modalism, Adoptionism, Macedonianism, Eusebianism, Subordinationism, Panentheism, Pantheism, and Eutychianism. I find it amazing that God used the Church — not the Bible or even Christ's explicit teachings — to reveal the Trinity, the greatest of all mysteries, the one most removed from the competence of the human mind, and correctly and infallibly to define and reject all alternatives, all heresies, and all misunderstandings of it, as orthodox (traditional, Evangelical, Biblical, Reformation) Protestants themselves admit.

• She has been right about Christ, avoiding both the Arian denial of His full divinity and the Docetist and Gnostic denial of His full humanity.

• She has been right about the Church, seeing herself both as a visible institution and as the people of God (not just the institution of God) and the Mystical (invisible) Body of Christ.

- She has been right about the sacraments, avoiding both materialism and spiritualism, both magic and mere symbolism.
- She has been right about Reformation Protestants, agreeing with their affirmations of "the faith once delivered to the saints" (Jude 3), which Catholics call Tradition with a capital T and the Deposit of Faith, and disagreeing with their infidelities to it and their negations of parts of it.
- She has been right about man, who is neither a god nor a beast, neither an angel nor an animal (nor both, like "the ghost in the machine"). She has avoided spiritualism, materialism, and dualism.
- She has been right about man being neither sinless nor saintless. She tells the most terrible sinners that they are called to become saints, and tells her saints that they are terrible sinners.
- She has been right about affirming both predestination and free will, affirming both halves of this most mysterious drama, and has avoided both Calvinism and Arminianism.
- She has been right about grace always being absolutely prior to nature and also validating, using, and perfecting nature rather than rivaling it or demeaning it. She has been neither Pelagian nor Ash'arite and Occasionalist. (Look 'em up!)
- She has been right about justification requiring both the root of faith (contrary to humanism) and the fruit of love, which means the works of love (contrary to Lutheranism).
- She has been right about morality, buying into neither Jansenist or Puritan rigorism and legalism, nor modern subjectivism, relativism, pragmatism, or utilitarianism.

- She has been right about seeing our enemies on both Left (Communism) and Right (Fascism).
- She has been right in opposing both totalitarianisms in the East (including Muslim ones today) and autonomous, libertine individualism, consumerism, and materialism in the West.
- She has been right about Islam being both a heresy and a noble religion that worships the same God as Jews and Christians but with crippling imperfection without Christ.
- She has been right about Judaism, in saying both that all Catholics are first of all spiritual Semites and that our command to preach conversion to Christianity is to all people, even our fathers in the Faith. And when our Jewish fathers in the Faith become Catholic, they always say they have become far more Jewish, not less, than they ever were before. Catholics are "completed Jews."
- She has been right about birth control, in the most unpopular encyclical in history. No one else in the world has been right about that.
- She has been right about divorce from the beginning. Christ clearly condemns and forbids it, and unlike all other churches, she has not arrogated to herself the authority to edit rather than deliver His mail.
- She has been right about the dignity and humanity of the body, against spiritualism, and the primacy and immortality of the soul, against materialism.
- She has been right about both the dignity of homosexual persons and the indignity of homosexual acts; about loving sinners and hating sins — both homosexual

and heterosexual sinners and both homosexual and heterosexual sins.

• She has been right about "the theology of the body,"
which is her balanced yet radical and surprising answer
to the primary and most destructive revolution of our
time, the sexual revolution.

In every challenge to her teaching, for two thousand years,
she has been as Chesterton describes her: a golden chariot on a
wild ride down the centuries through dangerous, narrow, rocky
mountain roads, always avoiding terrible abysses on each side,
careening wildly but never falling, reeling but erect, her captain
holding the reins of the wild horses, as all the heresies fall, on
every side.

Orthodoxy has been the exact and total opposite of what
most people mean by the name: not dull and obvious and hum-
drum and boring, like a comfortable suburban house, but a wild
adventure, in fact, the wildest, weirdest, most dangerous and
dramatic, most rollicking and romantic ride in history.

What does the history of the Church look like? A hymn describes it well and summarizes its cause in its first line. It's a love
story, with God incarnate as the heroic lover and the Church as
His damsel in distress:

> The Church's one foundation is Jesus Christ her Lord.
> She is His new creation by water and the Word.
> From Heaven He came and sought her to be His holy
>   bride.
> With His own blood He bought her and for her life He
>   died.
>
> Though with a scornful wonder, men see her sore oppressed,
> By schisms rent asunder, by heresies distressed,

Yet saints their watch are keeping; their cry goes up:
    "How long?"
And soon the night of weeping shall be the morn of song.

'Mid toil and tribulation and tumult of her wars,
She waits the consummation of peace for evermore,
Till with the vision glorious her longing eyes are blest,
And the great Church victorious shall be the Church at
    rest.

8

BECAUSE OF CATHEDRALS

Cathedrals are technological miracles, centuries ahead of their time. With their flying buttresses, they look like rocketships. They make your spirit fly. The miracle is that they do not fly off the ground themselves.

I would not be surprised to find, one fine morning, that they had all left their launchpads and taken off home to Heaven. Cathedrals are not just beautiful; they are unearthly (and yet utterly earthly, down to their gargoyles). They are the closest material approximation to Heaven that we have ever seen on earth.

They exist for one reason only: to be houses not for man but for God, for Jesus Christ, God incarnate, who is really present there in the Eucharist. Protestants do not build them, or if they do, it is only in imitation of Catholics.

I dare you: enter Chartres, or Notre Dame, or Westminster (which was originally built as Catholic), or St. Patrick's in New York. First, don't think, just look. Then, afterward, think: Where did they come from?

As the human face of a saint such as Mother Teresa shows forth visibly the invisible beauty of her spirit, so a cathedral shows forth the spiritual beauty of the Catholic Church, her *personality*.

Cathedrals are the miracle of stone and glass singing. I know three ex-atheists or ex-agnostics who were converted by Bach's *Saint Matthew Passion*. They instantly perceived that this music could not exist in a world without God. Cathedrals of music and cathedrals of stone and glass have the same power and make the same unanswerable argument. If you do not put up defenses, they are irresistible. To resist their upward gravity, you have to call upon the Devil's forces of downward gravity: cynicism, materialism, skepticism, nihilism, reductionism.

The origin and inspiration for these cathedrals very obviously came from Heaven. It's not hard to see that; it's hard not to see it.

Stop trying so hard!

9

BECAUSE THE CATHOLIC CHURCH IS NOT CHRIST'S ORGANIZATION BUT HIS ORGANISM, HIS BODY

I am a Catholic because the Church Christ founded and gave us is our literal, historical, temporal connector to Him. Without the connector, the wire that plugs into the infinite divine electricity, our souls die. We receive His life, His literal blood, through the umbilical cord of the Church's Eucharist. It literally incorporates us into His corpus, His body.

We also receive His mind through the Church's teachings. Infallible dogmas can come only from the only infallible mind in existence, the divine mind. But they do not save us; they are only the road map. Unlike Plato and Buddha, Jesus saved us by saying not "This is my mind" but "This is my body." And not just by saying it but by doing it, by giving us His body, on the Cross and in the Eucharist and in the Church. (It's the same body in

33

three places; Christ is not a monster who has three bodies, any more than He is a monster who has three heads.)

How do we make bodily connection with Him? It has to be bodily because we are bodily; that's why He became bodily, incarnate in time and space. He does not connect with us by taking us out of our bodies by mystical experiences. Christianity is not Hinduism or Buddhism. Christ connects with us where and when we are, here and now, and therefore in our bodies.

But time and space divide one body from another. There He is, two thousand years away in time on earth and infinitely far away in eternity in Heaven. How do we connect with Him? There He is, five thousand miles away in space on earth and infinitely far ontologically in Heaven. How do we connect with Him? You can't get to Heaven in a rocketship. "You can't get there from here."

He has to come to us. But how?

The connection can't be merely spiritual, by an out-of-body experience.

The Protestant answer is that it is by faith. Of course, we need faith, but not faith alone; we need faith's object, which is Christ. We don't have faith in faith (that's a hall of mirrors) but faith in Him. So, faith and an open heart are not enough, as hunger and an open mouth are not enough to be the solution to starvation; food is. Christ is our food; our faith is only our hunger and our open mouth.

So how do we get to Him? Rather, how does He come to us? Remember, it can't be merely spiritually, unless you are a Hindu rather than a Christian.

There is only one answer: He comes to us in His body today just as He came to us in His body two thousand years ago. And the Church is His body; it is "the extension of the Incarnation."

The body we receive in Holy Communion is the very same body that He saved us with by offering it on the Cross. He has only one body, but it is in three places: on the Cross, in the Eucharist, and in the Church. And He is in the Church in two ways, or two dimensions, because we exist in two dimensions and so does He in His humanity: He is in the public, external, objective, visible institution that teaches and sanctifies His people, and He is also in the private, internal, subjective, invisible souls and bodies of His people who are baptized into His body and who receive His body into their bodies in the Eucharist and who thus become the cells in His Mystical Body, the Church. When He said, "Unless you eat the flesh of the Son of man and drink his blood, you have no life [no *zoe*, no eternal, divine life] in you" (John 6:53), did He mean by His "flesh" His mortal body on the Cross, His sacramental body in the Eucharist, or His Mystical Body in the Church? Wrong question. It's not an either-or. Remember, He has only one body, not three.

To break with His body the Church is to break with Christ, just as to kiss or hit or heal or kill your body is to kiss or hit or heal or kill you. That's why St. Thomas More gave up his life over his king's break with Rome. (See the movie *A Man for All Seasons*; it's the most perfect movie ever made.)

10

BECAUSE ONLY THE CATHOLIC CHURCH CAN SAVE HUMAN CIVILIZATION FROM SPIRITUAL AND MATERIAL DESTRUCTION

Bodies—and the civilizations they make—follow souls wherever they go, both in this life and in the next, to Heaven or Hell. Whatever is good in the civilizations we make will be transformed and saved in Heaven. Whatever is not, will not.

- The Catholic Church is the only concrete thing in history, except for the Jews, that we know will still be here when Christ comes again and history ends, even if that is a million years from now. And when He comes, He will marry her (Rev. 21:2); and He is not a polygamist: He will not marry a harem of twenty thousand denominations.
- The Catholic Church is the greatest repository and synthesis of the wisdom of the past, and the only long-range hope for the future, of humane human civilization.

- The Catholic Church is immortal. Throughout history, whenever she seems to die, she rises. (See "The Five Deaths of the Faith," chapter 6 of Chesterton's The Everlasting Man.)
- The Catholic Church is the only thing in the world that wins even when she loses: the blood of her martyrs, shed in every age and most copiously in our own, is the seed that grows the most glorious fruits of the future Church.
- God incarnate promised that the gates of Hell would not prevail against His Church (Matt. 16:18), and I do not want them to prevail against me.

11

BECAUSE OF THE NOUNS

It's easy to offer verbs and adjectives and participles. But to offer nouns is to offer elephants.

Look at the size and weight of those nouns in the Catholic Church's theology: Father, Son, Spirit, God, Man, Eternity, Time, Good, Evil, King, Kingdom, Power, Glory, Heaven, Hell, Purgatory, Body, Blood, Soul, Immortality, Angel, Devil, Faith, Hope, Charity, Salvation, Sin, Life, Death, Saint, Savior, Lord.

Who dares to offer such nouns?

Who still dares to pronounce such heavy words in our hollow culture of paper-thin pop psychology with its "unbearable lightness of being," its fear of metaphysics?

Only the Church.

We have turned concrete nouns into abstractions or participles: *truth* into *truthiness* (Steven Colbert's brilliant satire), and *God* into *Divinity*, and *Man* into *Humanity*, and *mother* into *mothering*, and *father* into *fathering*, and then both of those into *parenting*, and *judgment* into *judgmentalism*, and *mind* into *mentality*, and *The Faith* into *faith*, and *good* into *appropriate*, and *substance* into *process*.

The Church's treasure house is full of unfashionable Things.

12

BECAUSE I WANT TO BELIEVE THE SAME THINGS THAT JESUS TAUGHT AND THAT HIS APOSTLES AND THEIR SUCCESSORS AND EVERY SINGLE CHRISTIAN IN THE WORLD BELIEVED FOR FIFTEEN HUNDRED YEARS

I want to believe the same things that all Christians believed until Protestant "reformers" started to cut branches off the tree of the Catholic Faith — truths that all Christians had believed for more than fifty generations:

1. The divine and therefore infallible teaching authority of the Church when she appeals to apostolic Tradition, the Deposit of Faith handed down from Christ

(of which Scripture is the chief but not the only aspect); that is, when she teaches theology or morality *ex cathedra* ("from the [teaching] chair" of Peter) and appeals to what Christians have always believed from the beginning (no *sola scriptura*)

2. The need for not faith alone (*sola fide*) but faith, hope, and love (i.e., charity, *caritas*, *agape*, which for Christians means not the feeling of love but "the works of love," to quote the title of a book by Kierkegaard, the greatest Protestant philosopher of all time); for, as George MacDonald, another great Protestant, pointed out, He was to be named "Jesus" not merely because He would save us from the *punishment* due to our sins but because He would save us from *our sins* (Matt. 1:21)

3. The principle that grace perfects rather than bypasses or minimizes nature, especially natural reason and free will (no *sola gratia*)

4. The appeal to Peter and his successors, the bishops of Rome (later called "popes") as the final authority ("Rome has spoken, the case is closed")

5. The fact that Christianity is essentially a social (i.e., ecclesiastical) religion; that we are saved by being incorporated into Christ's Mystical Body, not as individuals who then decide to "join a church" or "plant a church"

6. The historical fact of apostolic succession passed on sacramentally, which gives validly ordained priests the power to confect the Eucharist, i.e., to be God's agents in His changing (transubstantiation) bread and wine into the Body and Blood of Christ

7. The literal, full, Real Presence of Christ in the Eucharist

8. The power and authority of ordained priests in apostolic succession to be God's instruments in forgiving sins in the sacrament of Reconciliation (Confession)

9. The existence of Purgatory and the rightness of praying for the dead who are passing through there

10. The rightness of asking the saints in Heaven to pray for us, because of the Communion of Saints, the living connections among those who are in all three places where the Church lives: the Church Militant on earth, the Church Suffering in Purgatory, and the Church Triumphant in Heaven

11. The rightness of calling Mary "the Second Eve" and "the Mother of God" and "the Immaculate Conception," who was assumed into Heaven like Enoch and Elijah

12. The fact that all seven sacraments communicate divine grace to believers objectively and ontologically, *ex opera operato* (from the work worked), and not merely as aids to their personal faith

13. The infallibility and authority of the Church to define which books are Scripture (and thus divine revelation) and which books are not

I needed to believe all these things, not because I had figured them out for myself, but because the Church had always taught them, and all Christians had believed them, at least implicitly, and no one had ever denied them for fifteen hundred years, except for a few heretics, who were quickly labeled as such by the catholic (universal) church.

Then came a "reformation" that quickly became a revolution.

13

BECAUSE I WANT THE STRONGEST REASON TO BELIEVE THE BIBLE

St. Augustine says, "I would not believe the Bible but for the authority of the Church."

The Church wrote the Bible and defined (canonized) the Bible. That is, she was the efficient and formal cause of the Bible. How can a fallible cause produce an infallible effect?

History shows that all who have denied the infallible authority of the Church have eventually ended up denying the infallible authority of the Bible, too. About half of Protestants have already gone down that road and become modernists. The other half will eventually follow. For Bible and Church are a "package deal," because they are cause and effect, like father and son or chicken and egg.

It is the Bible that tells us that Christ founded the Church and endowed her with His teaching authority ("He who hears you, hears me" [Luke 10:16]).

It is the Bible that tells us that He gave the Church (His apostles) power to forgive sins.

It is the Bible that calls not itself but the Church "the pillar and bulwark of the truth" (1 Tim. 3:15).

It is not the Bible but the Church that defined the greatest of all mysteries, the Trinity, which all orthodox Protestants accept as divine revelation. It did that on the basis of the fivefold data in the Bible: that God is one; that the Father is God; that the Son is God; that the Holy Spirit is God; and that the Father, the Son, and the Holy Spirit are distinct Persons.

In exactly the same way, the Church defined the dogma of Purgatory on the basis of the threefold data in the Bible: that we are all sinners; that nothing sinful can enter Heaven; and that there is a very great gap between sin and holiness. Every Bible-believing Protestant I know who has read the *Catechism of the Catholic Church* has been surprised how biblical it all is.

History shows that we need the Church to interpret the Bible rightly, for every heretic in history has appealed to the Bible to justify his rejection of the Church. *Sola scriptura* has produced twenty thousand heresies, twenty thousand alternative churches: theological chaos.

I am a Catholic because I believe the Bible, and the Bible tells us that chaos is not the work of God.

14

BECAUSE OF WHAT THE CHURCH HAS *NOT* TAUGHT AS WELL AS BECAUSE OF WHAT SHE HAS

Two things the Church has not taught are: (1) which political system is best and (2) how divine grace and human free will work together. She does not know or claim to know these things with clarity and certainty, and neither should we.

Unlike Islam, the Church does not bless one form of government (Sharia) and curse all others. Thus, she refuses to succumb to the temptation to co-opt Christianity into service for a political party or system—any one.

It is tempting today to politicize your religion and to make a religion of your politics. But that is to relativize something absolute and to absolutize something relative. And it has never worked, whether in medieval or in modern times. When religion gets into bed with politics, she owes a debt to a whore.

Catholic social morality has some strong principles about politics, such as:

1. The principle of personalism (systems and things should serve persons, not vice versa)
2. The principle of the right to private property
3. The principle of the priority of the common good over the private good
4. The principle of subsidiarity (power should be dispersed, not concentrated, both because power corrupts and because smaller societies, such as families and neighborhoods, are closer to issues and problems than larger ones)

But these principles can be applied in many ways to different situations, different human capacities, and different human needs. We learn about which of these applications works best by trial and error, by experience, not by divine revelation.

Unlike Luther and Calvin, who deny free will because of their emphasis on "grace alone" and "the sovereignty of God," the Church does not deny human free will. And unlike Pelagianism and humanism, the Church does not deny the priority of grace and our total dependence on it.

Great books such as Augustine's *On Grace and Free Will* argue that these two things are *not* logically incompatible: (1) man's real freedom to choose good or evil, for or against God, and (2) God's sovereign, infallible grace (which includes both His totally altruistic goodwill and His omnipotent power and omniscient wisdom).

They have cast light on the issue and answered the charge that the two ideas are logically contradictory, but they have not eliminated the darkness surrounding the light. God, who is light, dwells in that darkness, which is, in fact, darkness only to us, but not to Him.

There are Catholic principles about providence, evil, free will, justice, and mercy, but (as Job discovered) we cannot deduce from them a clear insight into the mysterious divine plan by which evils are used for good (Rom. 8:28) and by which human gold is refined of its dross by the fire of suffering, since we see only a tiny bit of the process, not the final triumph. God's answer to Job was essentially the four words He preached to St. Catherine: "I'm God; you're not." The two most important principles He has given us in dealing with this great mystery are humility regarding ourselves and trust regarding Him, who is all wise, all loving, and all powerful.

The more I've thought about these two issues, the more I've admired the Catholic wisdom both for what it does claim to know and for what it doesn't.

15

BECAUSE OF ONE THING THAT I KNOW WITH CERTAINTY, THAT I DO NOT NEED BELIEF OR FAITH FOR

I know that I am going to die. The Church teaches me how to die.

Logic tells me that when I die, I will either (1A) not meet God at all, because He does not exist, or (1B) meet Him, because He does. And if He does exist, and I meet Him, I will either (2A) meet Him without Jesus Christ or (2B) meet Him in Christ. And if I meet God with Christ, I will do so either (3A) as a non-Catholic, without His visible Church and her sacraments or (3B) as a Catholic, as a member of His Church and with her sacraments.

Even if I cannot prove the three B options (and I think I can—but I could be wrong), Pascal's Wager tells me that B is a wiser choice than A each time.

1. My faith tells me that God exists, and my reason strongly supports that faith, but my reason tells me even more strongly that the stupidest faith of all is atheism. Not to prepare for the judgment on which my eternal life and happiness depend, or to prepare for it by making the atheist wager, is the stupidest thing I could ever do. It is like playing Russian roulette. It is like turning down a gift.

Let me put it in very crude terms: Faith is the gift of a free, eternal fire-insurance policy. Now this offer is either fake or true. If it is true, I gain everything and lose nothing. If it is fake, I gain nothing, but I also lose nothing.

2. The next question is: Do I meet God without Christ or with Christ, in Christ? If God is perfect, just, righteous, and holy, how dare I meet His gaze without Christ as my mediator and savior? Yes, God is merciful and loving and gracious, but I have often rejected His love and mercy and grace. I would have to be insanely arrogant to meet God without a Savior and a Mediator. It would be like falling into a fire without wearing asbestos clothing. If that sentence shocks you, I think you have learned your theology from pop psychology rather than from the Bible and the saints. As Rabbi Abraham Joshua Heschel said, "God is not 'nice.' God is not an uncle. God is an earthquake" (see Heb. 12:26–29).

3. The next question is: If I meet God as a Christian, will it be as a Catholic Christian, as one who is inside the Church, which is His body, having literally eaten His Body and drunk His Blood in the Eucharist, or will I meet God in a purely spiritual way, as a Protestant? When I look at my spirit, my soul, and when I look at my spiritual relationship with Christ, I am terrified at my weaknesses and proneness to all sorts of sin: pride, despair, greed for comfort, cowardice, lust, selfishness. These do not disappear

from my relationship with Him; and they are not like an external burden that I carry and can simply put down; they are inside of me; they are aspects of me. Only if I meet Him as part of His own body am I secure. I cannot fall through His fingers if I am one of His fingers. (That Catholic image is from the Dutch Protestant Corrie ten Boom.)

I therefore choose to accept the incredible gift of being incorporated into His corpus, His body, which is visible as well as mystical, sacramental as well as spiritual, by the means He made for us, which are also material and not just spiritual: Baptism, Confirmation, Confession, Eucharist, Viaticum.

I believe that this belief is not sheer belief, sheer faith, but is eminently reasonable. It is neither faith alone nor reason alone, but faith and reason married. Faith and reason are allies, not enemies.

16

BECAUSE GRATITUDE IS A NECESSARY PRECONDITION OF ALL RELIGION

Father Norris Clarke, S.J., my philosophy professor at Fordham, went to Tibet once, on his own, just to converse with the Buddhist monks there. After a day of delightful conversation with the Buddhist abbot about their religions, the abbot said, "Obviously, our two religions are very different. But I think they are also very similar in their root in the depths of the human heart. I would like to test this idea, with your permission. Here are four of my priests who speak good English. I will ask you and them the same question and compare your answers. I have never asked them this question before. The question is this: What is the first requirement for any religion at all?" Father Clarke thought that was an excellent experiment, so he agreed. He and the four monks wrote their answers on five pieces of paper. When the papers were unfolded and read, the very same single word was found on all five of them. The word was *gratitude*.

"That's very impressive," said Father Clarke. "But what do you Buddhists mean by *gratitude*?"

The abbot answered: "Gratitude for everything. For life, for death, for pleasures, for pains, for minds, for bodies—for everything."

"That is what I mean also," said Father Clarke, impressed. "But I have a question for you: If you do not believe in a God who created everything, then to whom are you grateful for everything?" The abbot said, simply, "We do not know." Father Clarke smiled, and said, "We do."

I am a Catholic because it would be insanely ungrateful for me to refuse the incredible gift Christ left us: His own body, by which He redeems the world—on the Cross, in the Church, and in the Eucharist.

How arrogantly ungrateful it would be for me to complain and draw back and be skeptical of the substance, the essence, of this gift because of the visible appearances of it. The Church looks like a ridiculously big zoo, complete with mounds of animal poop, but it is, in fact, the ark of salvation. The Eucharist looks like ordinary bread and wine, but it is, in fact, the Body and Blood of Christ. Jesus looks like any other merely human being, especially as He is dying on the Cross—but He is, in fact, God incarnate.

How arrogantly ungrateful it would be to refuse this Gift because of its shabby wrappings. If I accept the gift and open the wrappings, what do I find inside? Nothing less than the greatest gift ever given: Almighty God Himself, His own very life, which He wants to share with us and which He purchased for us at the price of His own infinitely precious blood. How can I possibly say: "What a disappointment! I wanted a puppy"?

Blood is very visible, very physical, very literal. It is not a mere symbol of something more spiritual.

Death is a very physical, crudely literal "problem." The Resurrection is a very physical, crudely literal "solution." The gift is physical. We are saved by Christ embodied, not Christ disembodied. He rose in the body. Where is that body now? Is it only in Heaven?

It is here. It is His gift. It is still being given. Accept it. Practice gratitude.

17

BECAUSE OF MY MOTHER

My mother on earth was not perfect, but she was 100 percent my mother, always there for me, whether by worry or by encouragement, but always by the gifts of love and charity: she willed to be my mother every day of her life.

The same is true of my mother in Heaven, Mary. She loves me and watches over me as any good mother does her child. She is 100 percent my mother, by her free choice and charity and by Christ's commission from the Cross: "Behold your mother" (John 19:27). She has a very large family.

The same is true of Mother Church. (Is Mary named after her, or is she named after Mary? Both.)

Like Christ, we have a Heavenly Father and an earthly mother. Like Christ, we have two natures, human and divine, if we are "born again" (John 1:13; 3:6). What God's angel said to Mary, he says to all Christians: "The Holy Ghost shall come upon thee, and the power of the Most High shall overshadow thee: therefore, also that holy thing which shall be born of thee shall be called the Son of God" (see Luke 1:35). Eternity enters time not only once, in Mary's womb, two thousand years ago, but whenever faith and Baptism happen. That is why the Church sees Mary as a symbol of Mother Church.

Mother Mary is the perfect saint. No one is simpler and humbler. Her whole self, her whole hope, her whole heart, her whole will is in a single word: *fiat*, "*let it be done* to me according to Your Word" (see Luke 1:38). Her whole message to us is contained in her words to the servers at the wedding feast at Cana when they ran out of wine: "Do whatever He tells you" (John 2:5). That is the simple essence of sanctity.

There is a metaphysical, cosmological, and psychological principle behind this practical ethic. It is the principle that power comes from humility. That is why Mary has more power over the Devil than any other creature has, and why he fears her so much.

But this humility is not just any humility and conformity, not just humility and conformity as such, but humility and conformity to God, to ultimate reality, to the nature of things, which necessarily reflect the nature of God.

Lao-tzu, in the *Tao Te Ching*, understood divine nature better than any other pagan ever did, though he did not know that that divine nature was lived by a divine Person, or, of course, that it was lived by three divine Persons. Lao-tzu's *Tao Te Ching*, Jesus' Sermon on the Mount (Matt. 5–7), and Mary's Magnificat (Luke 1:46–55) all say the same thing: that the "Tao," the "Way" the nature of all things works, the Way ultimate reality works, and therefore the way Christ, "the Way" (John 14:6), works, is not by power but by humility, not just by *making it be* but by *letting it be*, by His and our conformity to His Father's will, and therefore to the Father's nature and therefore ultimately to the nature of all things.

Chinese Bibles translate John 1:1 as: "In the beginning was the Way [Tao], and the Way was with God and the Way was God." Even though Lao-tzu did not know that this Tao, this Logos, was a divine Person, he knew a lot about the divine nature. It is Marian.

There is no reason Protestants should be leery of this. It's in the Bible!

18

BECAUSE OF THE ANGELS, AND THEIR INVISIBLE AND ANONYMOUS MEDIATION

God gave some angels (the guardian angels) to us "to light and guard, to rule and guide." Angels are there mediating most of God's great deeds in Scripture, and they certainly have a role in conversions. When I get to Heaven and meet my guardian angel, I will probably be shown his role in my conversion as well as in many other good things that have happened in my life, and I will be able to say to him, "Oh, so that was *you* all the time! Thank you!"

But when I say I am a Catholic because of the angels, I also mean something else: that from the standpoint of the angels, Catholics have it way over Protestants. Catholics are at home with angels. I don't know why Protestants usually aren't, but they aren't.

Catholic angels are *formidable*. They are as far from Hallmark greeting-card angels as Catholic saints are from Ned Flanders on

The Simpsons. They are not *fluffy*! They are not fantasies of human imagination but terrible and wonderful and forever unable to be adequately expressed in human art. Just as there has never been a really good movie about Heaven, so there has never been a really good movie about angels.

Some of our art gets closer to the real thing than others, but only the Catholic angels come close.

19

BECAUSE OF WHAT THE BIBLE TELLS ME

All Christians trust the Bible, including (especially) the New Testament. But the Bible leads me to the Church.

This happens in two ways. First, the Bible tells me that Christ established a Church and gave her His authority to teach in His name.

So, the Bible sends me forward to the Church, from Christ to His Church as His invention. The Bible also sends me backward to the Church, for the Church is its cause.

It is a historical fact that it was the Church (the apostles) that wrote the New Testament. It was also the Church that defined its contents, its canon — that told us which books did and which books did not belong in the sacred canon, the books that were divinely inspired and religiously infallible and authoritative. How else does any Christian know that the Gospel of Thomas and the Gospel of Judas are not part of the Bible, part of infallible divine revelation, and that James and Jude and Revelation are?

There is one and only one clear answer to that question: by the authority of the Church.

In other words, the Church was both the efficient cause (the author) and the formal cause (the definer) of the New Testament. That is historical data. Let that be premise 1.

But no effect can be greater than its cause (that is logically self-evident and indubitable), and the infallible is greater than the fallible; therefore, the infallible cannot be caused by the fallible. That is also logically evident. Let that be premise 2.

Either the Church is fallible or infallible. That is also logically self-evident. Let that be premise 3.

Therefore, if the New Testament is infallible, the Church must be infallible, and if the Church is not infallible, then the New Testament is not either. Logically, those are the only two possibilities, unless we deny either the historical data (premise 1) or one of the self-evident assumptions (2 or 3).

Go through it again. If the Church is fallible, as Protestants say, she cannot produce an infallible effect in the Bible. And therefore, if the Church is fallible, then the New Testament is also fallible, like its cause. On the other hand, if the New Testament is infallible, as both Protestants and Catholics say, then the Church, which was its cause, must also be infallible. Only if she is infallible can she produce an infallible effect.

Thus, we see in history what we would logically expect: that most of the "mainline" Protestant denominations have eventually abandoned the claim of infallibility for the New Testament and embraced modernist or liberal theology, for that is the logical conclusion of the denial of the infallibility of the Church. But never has the Catholic Church done so.

So, if I want to be an orthodox Christian and believe that the Bible is infallible, I have to be a Catholic and believe that the Church also has that divine gift. Church and Scripture go together, like body and soul.

I have probably offended modernist or liberal Christians in what I have said above about the Bible. I will now probably offend Fundamentalist Christians in what I will say below about the Bible. That's fine with me. Jesus also offended opposite extremes, opposite parties—the Pharisees and the Sadducees.

Fundamentalism denies the human nature of the Bible, and Modernism denies its divine nature, just as Docetism denies the human nature of Christ and Arianism denies His divine nature. That parallel is more than a coincidence, for both the Bible and Christ are called "the Word of God."

Here is my offense to Fundamentalists. The Bible is infallible in its religious teachings (and that includes morality, which is an essential part of religion for Jews and Christians), but not in its grammar or science or math. God did not give us the Bible to teach us grammar or science or math. The infallibility of the Bible does not extend to these things. It's simply a fact that there are some grammatical, scientific, and mathematical contradictions and errors in the Bible.

Now here's the point, the parallel between the Bible and the Church. The Church too is fallible in everything except her authoritative religious dogmas. The Church has taught some pretty stupid things, such as geocentrism, and done some pretty bad things, such as the Inquisition, but not infallibly, not authoritatively, not as Magisterium, or religious teacher. Popes have made mistakes, but not ex cathedra.

So once again the Bible and the Church are together. They are in the same boat. Each one sends you to the other one. If you want either one, you need the other. It's not *sola scriptura*.

Even after I figured out the logic of this argument, it was still hard for me to overcome either of my Protestant beliefs (1) that the Church was fallible and (2) that the Bible was not. But I knew, by reason, that I had to abandon one. So which was more certain to me: that the Church was fallible or that the Bible was not?

Was my faith more fundamentally anti–Catholic Church or pro-Bible? Once the question appeared that way, the answer was clear. When my faith and my reason thus married, they produced a Catholic baby.

20

I AM A CATHOLIC . . .

BECAUSE OF MY FRIENDS AND MY FAMILY — MY SPIRITUAL FAMILY

My friends and my family had a big role — largely invisible and unconscious, but partly conscious — in my journey home to Rome.

When I made the decision to abandon the spiffy new little lifeboat I was in and jump aboard Noah's big old ark, full of weird, smelly animals, I had a vision in my imagination of a kind of battle of the books, or rather, of the authors. From the windows of the ark I saw familiar faces peering out and inviting me aboard, faces that I greatly admired.

I had once (before I became a Catholic) listed the twenty-five authors in the fields of religion, theology, spirituality, and religious philosophy whom I loved and admired the most; and only two Protestants and two Orthodox authors were among them: C. S. Lewis, Kierkegaard, Dostoyevsky, and Tolstoy. Arrayed against them were twenty-one Roman Catholics: St. Justin

Martyr, St. Augustine, Boethius, St. Anselm, St. Francis, St. Bonaventure, St. Thomas Aquinas, Dante, Nicholas of Cusa, St. John of the Cross, St. Teresa of Avila, St. Catherine of Genoa, Pascal, St. Thérèse of Lisieux, Blessed John Henry Newman, G. K. Chesterton, Venerable Fulton Sheen, Frank Sheed, St. Teresa of Calcutta, and Ronald Knox. All these were waving to me from the ark and asking me why I had not come aboard to be with them and share their wisdom from its source rather than ungratefully consuming it from outside. I had no answer. My body and my mind said: Jump!

Eleven of the twenty-one were canonized saints. Good company, that. "A man is known by the company he keeps."

When you are in the ark, you are in a Really Big Family. Even when you feel alone, you're not. Even when you have no idea what to do or what to say, your spiritual relatives will help you, invisibly and anonymously, like the angels, if you ask them.

When you don't know how to pray, pray anyway, because your stupid words or lack of words, and your clumsy deeds or lack of deeds, will be made up for by your family, your friends in Heaven who see you struggling to pray and work and who are praying for you. You can draw on their spiritual "treasury" in Heaven just as you can draw on your biological family's resources on earth. They will supply their fuller, wiser, holier, more powerful heads and hearts and hands for your empty, stupid, sinful, weak ones. Their intercession is central to one of the twelve articles of the Apostles' Creed, the Communion of Saints, the one that Protestants have forgotten.

Why *shouldn't* this be so? Why should our religion be private instead of familial and social and communal? God is not a libertarian. Why should He be an autonomous individualist? He's not an American yuppie. Why should He be a Gnostic spiritualist?

He's not a Buddhist. Why should He be a Cartesian dualist? He's not a Protestant.

Christianity is essentially a social religion. We are not first saved as individuals and then invited into the Church; that is the Protestant picture. We are saved *by* being incorporated into the Church, the "ark of salvation," the holy family, the fellowship, the Communion of Saints.

The reason Christianity is essentially social is strikingly simple and absolute: because God is a social being, God is a Trinity, God is a family. And the nature of God is necessarily reflected in the nature of all reality.

21

BECAUSE OF THE PERSONALITY OF THE CHURCH'S SAINTS

Catholic saints are real characters. Catholic and Orthodox saints are much crazier and more memorable than Protestant saints.

They are unique individuals. No one could confuse St. Thomas the Apostle, Thomas à Kempis, St. Thomas Aquinas, St. Thomas More, and Thomas Merton. Or St. Teresa ("Mother Teresa") of Calcutta, St. Teresa of Avila, St. Thérèse of Lisieux, St. Teresa Benedicta of the Cross (Edith Stein), and Theresa your pious old landlady.

You can't argue with a saint. Their smiles, their charity, their wrinkles of experience and suffering and patience make your words bounce off them like stones thrown at battleships.

Saints are books, to be read. What do you read in them? The same thing you read in the Bible: Jesus. Saints are little Christs.

And what does Christ reveal? He alone reveals to us completely and perfectly the two things we most need to know: the nature of God and the nature of man; who God is and who we are—the two persons you can never escape or avoid for a single instant either in time or in eternity.

You understand Jesus a little better every time you meet a saint. And you understand the saints better when you know and love Jesus better.

When you meet a saint, you meet yourself: what you could be, should be, and in Heaven will be.

Why are Protestants (and even some modern Catholics) afraid of or embarrassed about the saints?

22

I AM A CATHOLIC . . .

BECAUSE ONLY THE CATHOLIC CHURCH IS MARKED OUT BY THE FOUR MARKS

The Nicene Creed identifies the Church of Christ by four marks: she is *one*, *holy*, *catholic*, and *apostolic*. Only one Church fits that description.

The description in the Creed is a description of our true home. It is a lighthouse, a roadmap, a clear marker for searchers and travelers.

One. Is any other church so *one* that all schisms that occur in that church are clearly schisms between the old and the new, between the Church that comes from Christ and one that comes from man, between the one Church that existed from the beginning and the breakaway group? The Catholic Church is the one church all other churches have to break away from.

Is any other church *one* through the ages, teaching the same dogmas, never going back on herself, never saying "oops" in matters of theological or moral dogma?

Is any other church *one* in space as well as time? Is any other church catholic, i.e., universal? As Chesterton says, how can a missionary ask an Outer Mongolian to become a Southern Baptist?

Apostolic. Is any other church *apostolic* in teaching both what the apostles taught and with the authority Christ gave to them and their successors? Is any other church *apostolic* in sacramental succession? Among Protestant churches, only the Anglican Church even *claims* apostolic succession, but they broke it when Henry VIII broke with Rome, with her bishops, and with her bishops' ability to ordain other bishops in the apostolic succession that began with St. Peter and always traced its lineage back to him.

Universal. Does any other church claim the name *catholic*, meaning "universal"? She is universal in many senses: for all men, for all the world, for all times, for all cultures, and teaching all that Christ and the apostles taught.

Holy. But what about *holy*? The Church contains many notable, even scandalously famous, sinners. A couple of them were even popes!

The Church's claim to holiness is not that Catholics are all holy people, or that Catholics are holier than other Christians. Her claim is that she herself is holy (*holy* means "set apart," implying "set apart by God"), and therefore the source of holiness. You can't give what you don't have: that is the principle of causality. The Church is the saint maker.

The meaning of life and the nonnegotiable divine command, which God repeated over and over again when He gave His law to His chosen people, is: "You shall be holy; for I the Lord your God am holy" (Lev. 19:2).

Christ did not mitigate this essential command but repeated it and made its absoluteness even more explicit, closing the door, the "escape clause," that we naturally add: "to the best of your ability—just try a little harder." He said: "You, therefore, must be perfect, as your heavenly Father is perfect" (Matt. 5:48). That is the reason for Purgatory. God will not take us out of the oven if we are only half-baked.

The Church is our connector with Christ. To break that connector is to break with Christ. To refuse the body is to refuse the Head. That is why St. Thomas More embraced martyrdom rather than approve Henry's break with Rome when Rome would not approve his divorce. Here is how he explained to his beloved daughter Margaret why he couldn't compromise his conscience just a little bit to save his life and the safety of his family, in *A Man for All Seasons*:

More. If we lived in a state where virtue was profitable, common sense would make us good ... and we'd live like animals or angels in the happy land that needs no heroes. But since in fact we see that avarice, anger, envy, pride, sloth, lust, and stupidity commonly profit far beyond humility, chastity, fortitude, justice and thought ... why, then perhaps we must stand fast a little, even at the risk of being heroes.

Margaret. But in reason! Haven't you done as much as God can reasonably want?

More. Well ... finally ... it isn't a matter of reason; finally, it's a matter of love.

Why does it take a Church (*the* Church) to make saints? Because we can't do it ourselves. We can't lift ourselves up by our own bootstraps. The physician can't heal himself. The tiger can't change his stripes.

But even though holiness is not a do-it-yourself thing, even though we need God and grace, why do we need the visible, concrete, historical, sacramental, material Church? Why can't our relationship with God and our dependence on God be one-on-one and spiritual?

Because Christ is not one-on-one and spiritual. Christ gathered an apostolic college, and founded a visible Church, and gave her His literal body and blood, both on the Cross and in the Eucharist. Catholics paint with His grain, not against it. Catholics just deliver His mail; they don't correct it.

God makes saints, but He does it through Christ, and Christ does it through His body, which is His Church.

Of course, it's done by the Holy Spirit, and it's spiritual. It's also done by Christ's incarnate body, and it's material. Why? Because it's done in man and for man, and man is not an angel but is always both spiritual and material.

To attain and achieve the meaning of life (of *your* life), be a saint.

To be a saint, go to Christ. To get wet, go where it's raining. To get holy, go where Christ is.

Where is Christ? In His body, not "out of the body." To go to Christ, go to His body, His Church.

Christ is in non-Catholics, too, spiritually, but not materially, not sacramentally, not Eucharistically. Why settle for a little lifeboat when you can have the whole ark?

23

FOR THE REASON WALKER PERCY GAVE: "WHAT ELSE IS THERE?"

When Walker Percy gave "What else is there?" as his reason for being Catholic, his interlocutor continued with something like this: "What do you mean, 'What else is there?' There are plenty of alternatives: fundamentalism, Modernism, left-wing liberalism, right-wing conservatism, materialism, spiritualism, pragmatism, idealism, classicism, romanticism, epicureanism, stoicism, utilitarianism, individualism, collectivism, relativism, male chauvinism, female chauvinism, unisexism, transgender-ism, transhumanism, pantheism, polytheism, Islamic terrorism, the Age of Aquarius, the New Age Movement, crystals, wicca, communism, neo-Nazism, anarchism, secular humanism (*fanatically* secular humanism!), narcissism, drugs, gangs, and the NFL."

Percy replied something like: "I rest my case."

His answer is biblical. When Christ taught about the Eucharist, most of His disciples left. He did not call them back and explain that they were wrong to take His words literally. Instead, He said to His disciples, "Will you also go away?" Peter replied as Percy did. (John 6:67–68, but read the whole chapter.)

24

I AM A CATHOLIC . . .

BECAUSE I AM GREEDY

When I find a good thing, I want more of it.

I used to be a Protestant. I still believe, love, and enjoy everything I believed as a Protestant and more. In fact, I am more Protestant—more evangelical, more charismatic, more biblical, and more Christocentric—as a Catholic than I ever was as a Protestant. (And that's in addition to all the things I have now that I didn't have then, such as the thirteen points in reason 12, above.)

It is exactly the same with Jews who accept Jesus as the Messiah and become Jewish Christians. They always say the same thing: "I am not less of a Jew but more of a Jew now. I am now a completed Jew, a total Jew."

I suspect the same is true of humanists: if they become Catholics they are more human than ever before.

Catholicism is very BIG. It's a religion with a lot of capital letters. If it's bad, that's very bad. (Hitler's Holocaust was bigger

81

and badder than Al Capone's.) If it's good, that's very good. (An archangel is bigger and better than an ant.)

So, Catholicism is among religions as Jesus is among human beings: either the baddest or the best; either subhuman or superhuman; either an arrogant, egotistic, lying, blasphemous false prophet or the one true church; either the Devil's or God's chosen vessel.

25

BECAUSE CATHOLICS, LIKE THEIR SAINTS, ARE A LITTLE CRAZY

In the words of a popular song, "How you gonna survive unless you're a little crazy?" But Catholic saints are more than a little crazy.

Their ideals, their passions, their loves, are tremendous, shattering, life-changing, radical. They show us our own suppressed hearts, as the great villains show us the suppressed villainy in us, the "Hitler in ourselves" (to quote the stunning title of a book by Max Picard, written right after World War II).

What, exactly, do they show us about ourselves and our hearts? One thing they show is that they and we are suppressed saints. There is a "good news–bad news" doubleness to this: on the one hand, it is to our credit that in our deepest selves we love and aspire to high and holy ends, but on the other hand, it is to our blame that we suppress and ignore these aspirations and settle for far lower ones.

Another thing the saints show us is that what they believe is likely to be true, not because they are clever or intelligent but because they are good. The coordinates and maps by which the ships of such lives are sailed are right, and therefore true. There is an argument here, an argument from goodness to truth, from will to mind, from sanctity to sanity. The two must be closely connected, for it is intolerable to think that the human heart is so badly designed and so self-destructively structured that its two absolute ideals, truth and goodness, contradict each other and lead us in opposite directions. How could one of these two greatest powers and innate desires of the human heart—for truth and for goodness—be right and the other one wrong? If so, which one is wrong? Which absolute must we betray in order to obey the other: honesty or holiness, wisdom or charity, truth or love, sanity of sanctity? Is sanctity a desperate attempt to attain goodness by ignoring truth? Are saints adults who act like little children playing games with invisible friends? Must we be cynical and selfish in order to be sane, in order to live in reality, in order to live in the real world? Was Machiavelli right and Jesus wrong?

Even in minor worldly matters, we naturally tend to think that what a good person believes is more likely to be true than what a bad person believes. How much more is this true, how much closer are these two values, the closer we approach to God Himself and to those (the saints) who resemble Him the most?

When you go down into the deepest depths of your own heart, you find these two equally absolute values as demands of conscience. If there is any natural revelation of the nature of God in the human heart, there it is. So, if both of these reflect God and if they contradict each other, that means that God too must contradict Himself. Are God and Satan two names for the same being? Does God have a dark side? If so, is it His dishonesty or His wickedness?

This argument defends all saints, not just Catholic ones, so it is not uniquely Catholic; but the Catholic saints confront us more wildly and challengingly, more powerfully and uncompromisingly with this argument than others, and it is especially apropos when those others judge Catholic saints as too extreme, too wild and crazy, as they usually do.

When God answered Job's complaint about the disorder and darkness in his life, God did not tone down or apologize for His wildness but pointed to it: Behemoth and Leviathan are not pets; they are monsters. But they are His monsters.

I think He was thinking of St. Francis of Assisi.

26

BECAUSE I KNOW I SHOULD TREAT OTHER PEOPLE AS IF THEY WERE CHRIST

The Church gives me the very best reason for treating other people as if they were Christ: because they *are*.

They are members of His body (1 Cor. 12:12–27). The English word *members* is misleading here. St. Paul is not using the analogy of membership in a club or a business or a secret society but in a *body*. Members of a body are *organs*. We are organs in His body. That's why He says, "Whatever you did for one of these least brothers of mine, you did for me" (Matt. 25:40, NABRE). He did not say, "I will count it as if you did it to me." He said, "You do for me." That's why He asked Saul, on the road to Damascus, "Saul, Saul, why are you persecuting *me?*" (Acts 9:4, NABRE).

That's why Mother Teresa was a saint. She believed this, and when she looked at another person, she saw Jesus Christ. And that's why you can be a saint too. All it takes is the vision of faith.

Do only Catholics have this vision?

Pretty much.

Protestants usually see the relationship between Christ and the Christian as legal and moral, personal and psychological, not metaphysical (see the next point, number 27), just as most of them see justification salvation as legal. (C. S. Lewis is more Catholic than Protestant here: see part 4 of *Mere Christianity*.) They say that salvation is just getting right with God (justification), not really becoming "a new creature" (2 Cor. 5:17), becoming a saint (sanctification); that faith alone saves you, not faith and works, the works of love; that God looks on you *as if* you were a saint and sends you to Heaven as long as you have faith in Christ; that you don't really have to be a saint to get to Heaven, just a believer; that Christ has fulfilled the requirements of the law for us, and that's why we get off.

In other words, God is a lawyer. Of all the blasphemous insults and heresies in history!

The word St. Paul uses most often for the relation between Christ and the Christian is the ineffably profound little word *in*. We are not merely *believers in* Christ and *disciples of* Christ and *lovers of* Christ and even *worshippers of* Christ; we are *in* Christ, and Christ is *in* us. Really! It is not a legal fiction; it is a metaphysical fact.

Pascal calls the Church "a body of thinking members."[1] In other words, you are Christ's little toe, and your neighbor is His thumb. Now you know how to treat your neighbor, and why.

St. Paul applies the same metaphysics to marriage in Ephesians 5:28–33 and explicitly parallels the one-flesh union between spouses with the union between Christ and the Church.

---

[1] Blaise Pascal, *Pensées* 482.

It is not just moral, emotional, and psychological; it is metaphysical. The two really do become one—one in being, not just in feeling.

That's the Catholic vision, and the one in the Bible. Protestants may have forgotten it, and swung over to modern subjectivism, but Catholics have not.

27

BECAUSE CATHOLICS STILL DO METAPHYSICS

Metaphysics is often misunderstood. It is not that division of philosophy that deals with the nonphysical or the supernatural; it is that division of philosophy that deals with being—all being, being as such.

A popular name for it is *worldview*. It means simply thinking about what is, and the real, essential nature of what is. It is as essential and as commonsensical as the child's question "What *is* it?"

All great ancient and medieval philosophers did metaphysics. Every one of Plato's dialogs begins with a metaphysical question: "What *is* that?" (justice, or friendship, or courage, or death, or love, or knowing, or virtue, or language). But contemporary philosophers tend to be skeptical of metaphysics because of pragmatism, positivism (scientism), historicism, utilitarianism, existentialism, materialism, subjectivism, and relativism, and above all because of Kant's skeptical epistemology, which denied that we can ever know "things in themselves" as distinct from appearances; and also because metaphysics cannot be done by the scientific method, which is in modern thought widely believed to be the only method that can give us certainty. (But the claim that "only the scientific method can give us certainty" is not provable by the scientific method. Like *sola scriptura*, it contradicts itself.)

The typically modern mind is not contemplative but practical, and does not seek or claim metaphysical foundations for its answers to the other kinds of questions that it prefers to ask—questions such as "What good is it?" or "What does it look like?" or "What does it do?" or "What can we use it for?" or "What does it mean to me?" or "What does it symbolize?" or "How does it make me feel?"

Catholicism is inseparable from metaphysics. Its fundamental claims are metaphysical.

An obvious example is the doctrine of the (objectively) Real Presence of Christ in the Eucharist, and the doctrine of Transubstantiation, the actual change in substance of bread and wine into Christ's Body and Blood, even though they appear not to. This requires the metaphysical distinction between substance (essential being) and accident (appearances).

Still another crucial example of metaphysics is the assertion that the sacraments really give us divine grace—in fact, that (as Scripture clearly says) "baptism ... saves you" (1 Pet. 3:21). It is more than a holy symbol or expression. It is not a work of art; it is a surgical operation on our souls.

Still another crucial example is the difference between Luther's "federal," or legal, theory of justification (that it does not change us metaphysically but only legally; God looks on us as holy even though we are not really transformed in our being, only in God's knowing) and the Catholic (and biblical!) notion that we must be really "born again" (John 3:3) from *bios* (natural life) to *zoe* (supernatural life, eternal life), from flesh (*sarx*: fallen, mortal human nature) to spirit (*pneuma*: human nature regenerated by the Holy Spirit).

Luther clearly confessed that he could not do metaphysics because he was a Nominalist. Nominalists reduce all universals (like justice, or substance, or being itself) to names (*nomina*), mere words. Luther called them a *flatus vocis*, "a fart of the voice."

Still another example of metaphysics is the Catholic and biblical assertion that we actually "partake of the divine nature" (2 Pet. 1:4). Catholics support this amazing claim and produce many mystics. Protestants tend to be skeptical of it, and of mysticism in general.

The fundamental claims of Catholicism are all metaphysical. The Church claims to know, by divine revelation, something about objective reality, not just personal experience. Catholicism is like science: universal and objective. Protestantism is more like practical psychology: individual and subjective.

Of course, Catholicism says a lot about personal experience too, about what is individual and subjective. It is big enough to include both. Its mentality is typically a both-and, not an either-or.

28

BECAUSE THE CATHOLIC CHURCH ALONE IN THE WORLD TODAY IS HARD WITH COURAGE IN A WORLD GROWN SOFT WITH SELF-INDULGENCE, CONSUMERIST AND SEXUAL

The Church is hard with courage in a world grown soft with self-indulgence. And she is soft with love and mercy in a world grown hard with pragmatists and numbers crunchers.

These opposite dimensions of her, the hard and the soft, are united in *sacrifice*, which offends the soft and fearful and the cowardly and self-indulgent by its demand for courage and also offends the hard and pragmatic and practical by its crazy idealism and unconditional love.

You see this in all her saints. Not one of them is simply soft or simply hard. Some are tougher than others, and some are tenderer than others, but not one of them is a coward or a moral relativist, and not one of them is an unforgiving legalist. The Church's male saints are all gentlemen: both gentle and manly. And her female saints are all strong women: both strong and womanly. Nobody else in the world today produces that. Instead, the men have become feminized and the women masculinized. They are either exchanging their sexual identities or losing them.

The Catholic combination of the hard and soft virtues, both in general and with respect to sexual personalities, is a combination that must be recovered to save our culture. For cultures go where people take them, and therefore without the saints, our culture will become either a *Nineteen Eighty-Four* jackbooted totalitarianism or a drug-dependent *Brave New World* cream puff. Or both. Walker Percy wrote, "It was compassion that led to the death camps." Hitler was sentimental.

29

BECAUSE I NEED DOGMATIC CERTAINTY ABOUT GOD, AND CHRIST, AND SALVATION

No Protestant denomination claims dogmatic certainty for itself. But we need it. We need not just probabilities or good opinions or good intentions on the road to Heaven, because our everything depends on this journey.

A mistake on other road maps may not be disastrous, but on this one it may, because death is final and there is no going back, no second chance.

But, on our own, we are not competent to know the truth about God, the way to Heaven, and the power to get there. We need divine, infallible certainty.

The Bible has that, yes, but twenty thousand Protestant denominations have twenty thousand interpretations of the Bible. There are not twenty thousand truths. We need *the* truth, not just *a* truth.

Christ is the Truth, yes, and all Christians believe in Christ, but which Christ? The merely human Christ, or the merely divine Christ, or the half-human but wholly divine Christ, or the half-divine but wholly human Christ, or the half-human and half-divine Christ, or what? Is He a human person with a divine nature, or a divine Person with a human nature, or what?

It was the Church who defined the answer to that question. It was the Church, not the Bible, who gave us the great Christological and Trinitarian creeds. (The words *Trinity* and *Incarnation* are not even mentioned in the Bible!)

If we cannot trust the Church, if the Church is not infallible like the Bible, then we may be trusting in twenty thousand Christs and worshipping twenty thousand Gods. That threatens not just our curiosity but our salvation.

Every heretic in history believed in and appealed to the Bible. History has proven that the Bible alone is not enough.

The reason it is not enough, the reason we need an infallible Church to interpret the Bible, is not Catholic arrogance but Catholic humility. We have dogma because God gave it to us, and God gave it to us because we need it, and we need it because we are not wise enough without it—not wise enough to interpret the Bible rightly without a divinely authorized teacher. For even though we have an infallible textbook, we are stupid students, and we need a wise teacher, a living teacher in the classroom of history to teach us the right interpretation of His textbook. If anyone denies that, it is he, not Catholics, who is arrogantly self-reliant and proud.

We need to be *certain* that our sins have been forgiven, and Jesus gave that authority to His apostles, who passed it on to their ordained successors.

We need to be *certain* that we are worshipping the real God and not a figment of our imagination or a construct of our own reason.

We need to be *certain* that we are really receiving Jesus Christ, and not just a symbol of Him, when we receive the Eucharist that He gave us.

We need to be *certain* that our creeds are infallibly true, since nothing merely human is infallibly true; and if the creeds are merely human, and not divine, they are not infallibly true. But the creeds are not in the Bible: the creeds come from the authority of the Church interpreting the data in the Bible. For instance, the Trinity is the Church's single interpretation of the six main pieces of data in the Bible, which tells us (1) that there is only one God; (2) that the being whom Jesus calls His Father is God; (3) that Jesus is God (He accepted the title from "Doubting Thomas" [John 20:28]); (4) that the Holy Spirit is God; (5) that Jesus is not the same Person as His Father (since He obeys His Father's will); and (6) that the Holy Spirit is not the same Person as Jesus or the Father, since Jesus and the Father "send" Him.

We need to be *certain* that God loves us, and therefore we can trust Him for absolutely everything, for that idea is almost literally too good to be true and seems almost certainly to be wishful thinking.

We need to be *certain* that death is not the end. Philosophical arguments are not enough. We need more than the "hope" that is mere optimism or probability; we need "the *sure and certain hope* of the Resurrection" (Catholic graveside burial prayer).

We need to be *certain* that our loved ones who die have not just "passed away." We need more than human love and sympathy and the nostrums of pop psychology. Because death is certain, we need our answer to it to be even more certain.

We need to be *certain* that we are not arrogantly claiming a certainty that we know, deep down, we do not have, or have a right to. We need to be certain that our Faith is God's dogma, not our dogmatism.

30

I AM A CATHOLIC . . .

BECAUSE ONLY THE CHURCH CAN WHUP THE DEVIL

Whenever anybody gets really serious about exorcism, they go to a Catholic priest. Did you ever see a movie with a Protestant exorcist?

The Catholic Church is an "expert" in the most dangerous war of all, spiritual warfare. Why? For these reasons:

1. Jesus was. He performed many exorcisms in the Gospels. And His Church does His work.
2. She has the experience of two thousand years of this work.
3. She has the supernatural power to do this work, given to her by the Holy Spirit.
4. The Devil is an "expert" at attacking his holiest and most formidable enemies.
5. Almost nobody in our culture today believes the Devil even exists anymore, and in any war, ignoring

your enemy makes him invisible and ten times more powerful.

6. Natural weapons alone are insufficient against a supernatural enemy.

7. We have a nuclear arsenal in Mary, who is more powerful in gently protecting her beloved children than the Devil is in attacking them.

8. The Devil loves to target women and children, especially in our culture today.

9. The Devil really, really resents being smashingly whupped by a woman, especially a womanly woman, holy and humble and (therefore) happy instead of an Amazon full of anger and resentment and belligerence like himself. Just look at all Mary has done in recent history, from Guadalupe to Fatima and Zeitoun. (Never heard of it? Google it.)

31

I AM A CATHOLIC...

TO SAVE CIVILIZATION FROM ITS ENEMIES

Satanists, Marxists, porno billionaires, worldwide conspirators, neo-Nazis, terrorists, and disciples of the Marquis de Sade hate and fear the Catholic Church more than anything else in the world. In one way, they are wiser than Protestants; they recognize who she is: their worst enemy.

Why did the Roman empire target only Jews and Christians for torture and elimination? Because the Devil isn't stupid. He knows who his real enemies are.

Imagine what kind of world we would have without the Church. Imagine pagan Rome lasting until modern times. It would be almost as bad as Hitler's "thousand-year Reich." Or worse.

Even Protestants need the Church. If the Church didn't exist, they would lose their identity. What would the "protesters" protest against?

If they answer that their identity is not essentially negative and protesting, but positive, the reply is that Catholics already believe all the same positive things Protestants believe, and more. All the differences are differences between what we believe and what they don't.

The Church fought and conquered paganism, polytheism, heresies, fanatical sects, slavery, totalitarianism, genocide, the legalized murder of innocent unborn children, the sexual revolution, and all the other false religions that have risen against her. Yes, all those things are false *religions*, false absolutes, unlike ordinary perennial sins, such as theft, adultery, greed, oppression, or hard-hearted legalism. They had (and have) a religious passion behind them.

We are at war, and have been ever since the snake sneaked into the garden. Stop and smell the gunpowder. Those rocks you are skipping over are land mines and those butterflies around your head are bullets. If you don't believe that, ask an angel.

The Church on earth labels herself the Church Militant, even though she often looks more like the Church Mumbling.

The heart of the war today is about sex. Nearly every rebellion against the Church today is about sex and sexual morality. It is the chief engine for moral relativism. Did you ever hear anybody defend murder? Only if it is in the name of sexual "freedom." Its name is abortion. Why does any woman want an abortion? Because other methods of contraception failed. What is contraception? The demand to have sex without having babies. Did you ever hear anybody defend child abuse? Only if it is in the name of sexual "freedom." Its name is divorce.

I am a Catholic because only the Catholic Church has the full, definitive, big-picture answer to the most destructive revolution of all time, the one we are living through today, the *first* sexual revolution, which is decimating the lives (literally, by abortion) and the happiness of children and destroying the single most essential building block of all stable societies, namely families. That answer is St. John Paul II's "theology of the body." That is the *second* sexual revolution, and the true one.

The Church has always been countercultural about sex, and always right. It's an old battle, not a new one; but it's in its most crucial and radical stage today, the stage just before "Brave New World."

32

BECAUSE OF THE MOVIES

Hollywood knows that the alternative to secularism and materialism and skepticism and agnosticism and atheism and nihilism is Catholicism.

Whenever they make a serious movie and religion is in it, it's always a Catholic church and a Catholic priest that they use.

33

BECAUSE WHEN I GO TO CONFESSION I WANT TO BELIEVE THAT ADAM WALKS INTO THE CONFESSIONAL AND JESUS WALKS OUT

When I look at a crucifix, and realize who that is, what He is doing, why He is doing it, what it cost Him, and whose sins made all that necessary, I realize the weight of sin — of my sin — and how absolutely I need to divorce myself from my divorce from God. I know I need a miracle, not a happy face.

I need to know that Jesus has saved me not just from the punishment that justice demands for my sins, but also from my sins. What a selfish, low, calculating idea it is to call Him "Jesus" (that is, "Savior") only because He saves me from the *consequences* of my sin (death and Hell).

God decreed, through His angel, that His name shall be called Jesus because He shall save His people from their *sins* (see Matt. 1:21). I don't just want legal protection; I want an operation. I don't just want amnesty; I want surgery. I want to be clean.

I am a Catholic because even the most liberal, modernist, skeptical, minimalist, "enlightened," desupernaturalized compromiser, when his conscience wakes up, wants the traditionalist, conservative, orthodox, supernaturalistic, dogmatic dogma about the sacrament of reconciliation to be literally true: that when the priest claims divine authority to forgive sins, he really has it.

34

BECAUSE I DON'T WANT TO LIVE IN A ONE-PARENT SUPERNATURAL FAMILY

I need a Mother in Heaven as well as a Father.

Jesus had a divine Father as well as a human mother; a Heavenly Father as well as an earthly mother. I need the same. The Christian is to be "a little Christ"; therefore, the Christian needs a divine Father as well as a human spiritual mother: Mary.

We all need the unique instincts and wisdom and sympathy and hidden power of mothers. This is how God designed human nature. Human nature was designed in Heaven, not in Hollywood or at Harvard. It did not come from us; it *is* us. Its essential properties are not relative to culture, historical time, psychological profile, or denomination. And motherhood is one of its essential properties.

Our culture is gravitating more and more toward a Brave New World in which a cultural Skinner Box replaces motherhood.

The Church is more focused on Mary today than ever before because we need her more today than ever before.

She has many titles, but her primary and essential one is "mother," "Blessed Mother," "Mother of God."

Mothers are inclusivists. They bring people together, because they have known togetherness with another person (their un-born children) more intimately than any man can ever know. Mary includes all possible relationships with God, with all three divine Persons, perfectly: daughter to the Father, mother to the Son, and spouse to the Spirit. All three of those relationships are in crisis in our culture in the lives of women.

The Church not only gives our culture its answer in Mary; she also gives me my answer in Mary. All I need to know is her wisdom, and her wisdom consists of just one word: *fiat* (Luke 1:38; or, the slightly longer version: "Do whatever He tells you" (John 2:5), because that wisdom *is* just one Word, the Word of God, to whom she is totally transparent. The Protestant fear that Mary will draw me away from Christ is exactly as reasonable as the fear that Christ will draw me away from the Father. Mary's whole passion and work — exactly 100 percent of it, with not an iota left over — is to direct me to Christ, to unite me to her divine Son. And she will not rest until by her powerful love and intercessory prayer she has made every one of her many children into little Christs.

35

BECAUSE I NEED PURGATORY

When I die, what are my possible alternatives to Purgatory?

1. That I am holy enough to endure Heaven, the direct vision of the infinitely holy fire of divine justice? It is more likely that I could climb Mount Everest on my knees in my old age.

2. That I go to Hell instead, even though I love Jesus and Jesus loves me? Why would He allow that?

3. That I be reincarnated? But the Bible says that "it is appointed for men to die once, and after that comes judgment" (Heb. 9:27).

4. That I never die but live on earth forever in this decaying corpse of a body? Biologically impossible and psychologically unendurable.

5. That I simply cease to exist? But I am made in God's image, and my soul is immortal.

There is simply no alternative for me.

And it is only the Catholic Church that teaches and, in a sense, "administers" Purgatory, through her prayers in the Communion of Saints. She is my hope because Purgatory is my hope. And Purgatory is my hope because she is my hope.

Purgatory is infinitely more joyful than painful because everyone in Purgatory is absolutely certain that they are guaranteed "graduation" to Heaven, which we cannot be absolutely certain of that in this life; and also because God is there in a way that is also more certain and more indubitable, holding our hand through all the painful re-education that we need, and that we will perceive we need, and that we will desire with all our heart. Thus, we will get what our heart desires, and we will not be frustrated but satisfied and thus happy, even in our pains.

Purgatory is not an alternative to Heaven, a third possible eternal destiny in addition to Heaven and Hell, but a part of Heaven (the temporary part, the bathroom), and that is why it must be full of joy as well as pain. Pain is not *evil*, like sin, so it is possible that there can be pains in Heaven. But they are good pains, and we will be wise enough to want them and embrace them, so we will get what we want.

If you do not understand this, think of a remote analogy. Have you ever been constipated for a long time and then suddenly needed a long visit to the bathroom? If so, you know something of the joys of Purgatory. Or, if you have a good imagination, imagine you are a snake and need to take off your old, hard, dirty, constricting skin and find a new, soft, beautiful one underneath.

When I die, I will be judged as God's child in Christ, and I will enter Heaven. And when I show up at the front door of His Heavenly mansion with my soul dirty and disheveled by sinful habits that are still in my personality, my character, even though God has remitted His just punishments for all my deeds, I think He will say to me, as He leads me through the door, "My dearly beloved child, for whom my Son died, you are infinitely welcome to my banquet. But before you sit down at the dining-room table, would you not like to take a good hot cleansing bath first? For you are full of dirt, and dung, and bugs. In fact, you *stink*. I love you infinitely dearly, even beneath all that filth. But I cannot embrace filth. I cannot love you as much as I want to, and you cannot embrace me as you want to, until your filth is removed." Would you not beg Him for that bath?

But it will hurt your soul in its pride and self-satisfaction and fears and cowardice and comfort-mongering. It will hurt because it will reveal the horror of all your sins and all the harm they did to Him and to those you love, and because it probably will cauterize your body, too. But you will plead for that hot bath, with all its fires and pains. Fire, remember, gives us not only heat but also light. We need to see, we need to know the truth, even the "bad news" truth. That is why Hell must exist: so that no one lives forever in illusion. Hell is truth known too late.

St. Catherine of Genoa, to whom God gave supernatural visions of Purgatory, says that (1) because sin is far worse than any other evil, the pains of Purgatory that deal with our remaining sinful habits and desires are far greater than any pains on earth, but also that (2) the joys of Purgatory are also far greater than those of earth because God is with you and you know that you are absolutely guaranteed eternal salvation and incomprehensible ecstasy with Him forever. And (3) the degree to which the joys of Purgatory are greater than the joys of earth is itself far greater than the degree to which the pains of Purgatory are greater than the pains of earth.

When I became Catholic, my father was very upset. He was a good, wise, holy Calvinist, and we had a lot of theological arguments. One of them was about Purgatory. My mother was listening, and after a half hour of listening to my father and me arguing and getting nowhere, she interrupted.

"John," she said (my father's name was John), "if I understand Peter, he's just saying what the Bible says."

"Of course he's not," my father answered. "He's defending Purgatory. Purgatory isn't in the Bible."

"Well, maybe not, but I think the only reason he believes in it is because he believes the Bible. Peter, here is what I hear you saying. Tell me whether I'm right. The Bible says that we're sinners: 'If we say we have no sin, we deceive ourselves and the truth is not in us' (1 John 1:8). And the Bible tells us that nothing sinful can enter Heaven (Rev. 21:27). And the Bible tells us that there is a total difference between sin and holiness (1 John 1:5). So God has to do *something* to us when we die to change us from sinners into saints, and if the Catholics want to call it Purgatory and we don't, aren't we arguing only about words?"

My father was silent. "Well, maybe so. Let's talk about the other stuff."

36

I AM A CATHOLIC . . .

BECAUSE, AS ST. THOMAS AQUINAS SAYS, NO MAN CAN LIVE WITHOUT JOY

St. Thomas Aquinas says that no man can live without joy. (He goes on to say, "That is why those who are deprived of true joy go over to carnal pleasures." I never read a more profound analysis of the origin of sexual addiction.)

Joy comes from God: real joy, true joy, what Augustine calls "joy in truth," deep, authentic, lasting joy, joy that is not ephemeral and not merely emotional or sentimental and subjective, and not merely external and physical and animal. Pleasure gets boring, and so does even happiness (contentment, the satisfaction of our desires), but joy never gets boring.

Jesus is the only Person in history who never bored anybody.

The commonsense principle of causality says that you can't give what you don't have. God alone gives us this joy, because God alone has it by nature, eternally. It is a dimension of His own divine life, and He wants to share it with us through Christ, who is the only way anyone on earth, at any time and in any place or culture or religion, can ever be really connected to God, to the true God.

What does this have to do with Catholicism? Everything. For Christ gives it to us through His body, the Church, into which we are incorporated. Augustine says, "By receiving the Body of Christ, we become the Body of Christ." That is why being a Catholic is life's supreme joy, and life's greatest adventure.

Roquentin, Jean-Paul Sartre's nihilist protagonist in his novel *Nausea*, says: "I have never had adventures. Things have happened to me, that's all. It's not just a question of words."

37

BECAUSE THE HOLY SPIRIT IS THE SOUL OF THE CHURCH, AND I NEED THE HOLY SPIRIT TO "HAUNT" ME WITH THE VERY LIFE OF GOD

We need to be "possessed" by the Holy Spirit. It is the exact opposite of being possessed by an evil spirit: it makes us free and clean and full of joy.

Receiving the Holy Spirit is the last and fullest stage of intimacy with God. God is love, and what love seeks is intimacy, personal union with the beloved. That is why God revealed Himself in three stages. They are the stages of intimacy: first as the interfering love of the Father in the Old Testament, then as the brotherly love of the incarnate Son in the Gospels, and finally as the Spirit of love in the history of the Church (God outside us, God beside us, and then God inside us).

Because the Holy Spirit is the final stage of God's intimacy with us, we need Him for maximal joy, and we find Him in the Church, for He is "the very soul (life) of the Church."[2]

The Holy Spirit is the love between the Father and the Son. Just as the Father's knowledge of Himself is so real that it is a Person, eternally and spiritually "begotten" by the Father, so the love between Father and Son is so real that it is also a Person, eternally "proceeding" from Father and the Son.

The Holy Spirit is too real to be anything but a Person. This presumes that there are degrees of reality, that not everything is equally real. Lies are not as real as truths. Fictions are not as real as facts. Quantities (such as the number 5.4) are not as real as qualities (such as wisdom). Abstractions (such as wisdom) are not as real as concrete things (such as a wise man). Evil is not as real as goodness (for it is a hole in goodness). No creature is as real as the Creator (for of itself it does not have existence, as He does; it needs to be created). And nothing is as real as a person. That is why God is three Persons, not a force or an ideal or an impersonal mind or will. (Minds and wills are dependent on persons, are found only in persons, and are powers of persons.)

The Holy Spirit is not something abstract, such as "the spirit of democracy" or "school spirit." He is a concrete Person. (Here, *concrete* does not mean "material" but "individual." St. Michael the Archangel, who is a pure spirit without a material body, is concrete; but mud, or rock, as distinct from this mud ball or this rock, are abstract.)

And He offers Himself to our souls spiritually (all three divine Persons do) through the material sacraments of His Church. And when He lives there in our souls, we are full of joy and we

[2] John Paul II, General Audience, July 8, 1998.

are unconquerable, because we live in, and become part of, the very love that holds the Trinity together more strongly and in a more unified way than arithmetical and logical identity can do. (Even among us, the love that makes two lovers who give themselves wholly to each other ("one flesh") makes a greater unity, a stronger glue, than the force that holds each one together as a single person, for either one would die for the other, which shows that each is more "attached" to the other than to self.

That love that is the very life of God is stronger than hate, stronger than sin, stronger than death. Death separates us from ourselves (for we are both body and soul, and death separates body and soul) and interjects into our being the nonbeing, the nothingness, that is the life of the Devil. He is "the prince of this world" (see John 16:11). But the very life of God is in us through Christ and His Church, and therefore "he who is in you is greater than he who is in the world" (1 John 4:4). If we are in Christ, the Holy Spirit is to our soul what our soul is to our body: its transcendent (and immanent) life.

38

BECAUSE THE CHURCH DEFENDS ALL OF GOD'S CREATIONS AS WELL AS THE CREATOR

The Church defends nature as well as grace, because she believes that grace perfects and redeems and loves and validates nature instead of dispensing with it, minimizing it, bypassing it, or rejecting it. There are dozens of examples of this key Catholic principle:

- The Church defends man as well as God, for God has become man, and the second Person of the Trinity is a man as well as God forever. The Ascension was not the undoing of the Incarnation. Jesus did not leave His human body or soul behind.
- The Church defends reason as well as faith. It is matter of faith, as defined by Vatican Council I, that God's

existence can be proven by reason and is not merely a matter of faith!

• The Church defends the body as well as the soul, for the two are one, like the meaning and the words of a book.

• And because the Church defends the body as well as the soul, she defends not just the human soul of Christ but also His body, and the extension of His body in the Church. And in the Church, she defends both the Head (Christ) and the body (us).

• The Church defends matter as well as spirit, for He created both. From her earliest times (the times of the Gnostic heresy referred to by St. John in his first epistle) to today she has opposed Gnosticism, or spiritualism (Chesterton calls "spirituality" "a dreadful doom").

• She defends the state as well as the Church (it's all in St. Augustine's City of God).

• She defends natural loves as well as supernatural loves (see C. S. Lewis's Four Loves and Pope Benedict XVI's uniting of eros and agape in Deo Caritas Est).

• She defends secular literature as well as the Bible. (There have been far more Catholic novelists, poets, and artists than Protestant ones.)

Grace always loves, protects, defends, perfects, sanctifies, uses, and glorifies nature. The principle is obvious—and glorious. And it is theologically true because God is love, and love loves and perfects the beloved.

The Protestant tendency has always been an either-or (as in Kierkegaard's great title), while the Catholic tendency has always been a both-and: both grace and nature, in all the examples above.

Even the dispute between the Protestant either-or and the Catholic both-and is a both-and rather than an either-or for the Catholic, for the Catholic spirit makes room for the Protestant either-or (e.g., Heaven or Hell, good or evil, faith or sin, yes or no to God) but the Protestant either-or is suspicious of the Catholic both-and.

39

I AM A CATHOLIC . . .

BECAUSE I VALUE REASON

I mean two things by this. One is that my reason impels me to be a Catholic; that Catholic apologetics "works." The other, deeper, and more important thing is that Catholicism broadens my reason. For the object of modern "reason" is not being, not reality, but Cartesian "clear and distinct ideas" and arguments.

And among arguments, the objects of modern reason are arguments whose validity can be determined by a computer, using mathematical logic, while the object of reason in the older, Catholic sense is wisdom, intelligence, intellectual intuition, insight, or understanding, whose natural object is great ontological mysteries.

The Church shows us what reason really means at its highest. It is ancient, it is big, it is metaphysical, not mathematical. It is at home in the most mysterious things of all—which are the great mysteries of life—whereas modern reason is at home in the least mysterious things of all, which are numbers. Numbers are the only totally clear and unambiguous language in the world, and the least profound and interesting. What it says, it says very clearly, but what it says is barely worth saying.

I am very sympathetic to modern atheists and agnostics who perceive that Catholicism is full of astonishing and barely believable mysteries:

- That this institution that claims to be divinely authorized looks "human, all too human"
- That that stuff on the altar that the Church claims is the literal Body and Blood of God Incarnate looks to all appearances and all scientific tests like ordinary bread and wine
- That in this religion, the God who is the infinitely perfect being, who can have no possible needs, nevertheless loves His rebellious creatures so much, despite their stupid, selfish, shallow undeservingness, that He goes to ridiculous and inconceivable lengths to redeem them
- That in this religion, these fleshly creatures are raised above the angels, who are morally and ontologically pure spirits, and are destined to participate in the very divine nature in the Beatific Vision, of which the highest possible mystical experience in this life is but a tiny appetizer

It's *crazy*.

God's love is a crazy love.

It's ridiculous.

I sympathize with those who see that and whose reason drives them away from this thing that surely seems much too good to be true. I sympathize with those who feel that, but only as long as they also have hearts that move them in the opposite direction and make them at least wish it were all true — in other words, those who have something like hope even though they have nothing like faith. What I have no sympathy for is those who do not see this crazy fairy tale as anything more than dull, moralistic platitudes and repression of human joy. They are not looking at the Faith through any glass window, however darkly; they are looking at themselves and their own hearts in a mirror.

40

BECAUSE JESUS IS THERE, IN THE CHURCH, IN HIS BODY

And that is where I meet my Lord and my God, my absolute and nonnegotiable All.

He is present everywhere, of course, in some way; but *presence* is not univocal; there are different kinds and degrees of it. He is present in Himself more than in any creature; He is present in creatures with rational souls more than in any other kind of creature; He is present in good and loving people and in good and loving deeds more than in bad ones; He is present in the baptized, the believing, the saved, those (known clearly to God alone) who are in the state of grace more than in those who are not. He is present in the Church's seven sacraments more than in sacramentals (such as holy water and icons) even though He is present in everything sacramental and, in some sense, everything is sacramental; and He is present in the Eucharist as fully and truly as He was in the dusty streets of Jerusalem and on the bloody splinters of the Cross.

That little red sanctuary light is the candle in the window of my home, the glowing embers of the fire in the fireplace of my living room, the only room I can truly live in. He is the fire. The Church is the fireplace, the place where there is that fire. That is what every dogma, every moral law, every sacrament, every prayer, every sermon, every Bible, every hymn, every molecule in every pew in every church building, and even every penny in the collection plate are all about: that fire, that Person.

If that's *not* true, if the Church is merely a human organization and not a divine organism, then it's the world's most elaborate and absurd lie, trick, fallacy, fantasy, fiction, or practical joke, and, to quote Flannery O'Connor, I say, "the Hell with it all."

But if it *is* true, I say, to the body as well as the Head, "My Lord and my God."

Protestants see that as idolatry. Why are they wrong? Because this body is not headless, and this Head is not bodiless.

Sophia Institute

Sophia Institute is a nonprofit institution that seeks to nurture the spiritual, moral, and cultural life of souls and to spread the Gospel of Christ in conformity with the authentic teachings of the Roman Catholic Church.

Sophia Institute Press fulfills this mission by offering translations, reprints, and new publications that afford readers a rich source of the enduring wisdom of mankind.

Sophia Institute also operates two popular online Catholic resources: CrisisMagazine.com and CatholicExchange.com.

Crisis Magazine provides insightful cultural analysis that arms readers with the arguments necessary for navigating the ideological and theological minefields of the day. *Catholic Exchange* provides world news from a Catholic perspective as well as daily devotionals and articles that will help you to grow in holiness and live a life consistent with the teachings of the Church.

In 2013, Sophia Institute launched Sophia Institute for Teachers to renew and rebuild Catholic culture through service to Catholic education. With the goal of nurturing the spiritual, moral, and cultural life of souls, and an abiding respect for the role and work of teachers, we strive to provide materials and programs that are at once enlightening to the mind and ennobling to the heart; faithful and complete, as well as useful and practical.

Sophia Institute gratefully recognizes the Solidarity Association for preserving and encouraging the growth of our apostolate over the course of many years. Without their generous and timely support, this book would not be in your hands.

www.SophiaInstitute.com
www.CatholicExchange.com
www.CrisisMagazine.com
www.SophiaInstituteforTeachers.org

Sophia Institute Press® is a registered trademark of Sophia Institute.
Sophia Institute is a tax-exempt institution as defined by the
Internal Revenue Code, Section 501(c)(3). Tax I.D. 22-2548708.